Letts

CW01652400

Maths BASICS

FOR AGES 7-8 KEY STAGE 2

Contents

Place value 3
Addition and subtraction 4
Word problems: addition and subtraction 5
2D shapes 6
Numbers: counting and properties 7
Multiplication tables 8
Money 9
Fractions 10
Time 11
Data handling 12
Rounding and scales 13
Addition 14
Word problems: multiplication and division 15
3D shapes 16
Measures and time 17
Numbers: odd and even 18
Multiplication and division 19
Money 20
Fractions 21
Data 22
Place value and rounding 23
Subtraction 24
Money problems 25
Shape: right angles 26
Counting and estimating 27
Division 28
Problems 29
Fractions 30
Time 31
Data 32
Answers

How to use this book

Numeracy Basics helps you to help your child practise many important basic skills covered in the *National Numeracy Strategy* and *National Curriculum*.

Each book is divided into *30 units* of work which focus on *one clear* objective.

Most of the units are designed using the same easy-to-follow *key features*. In some cases these features are combined into one activity, offering further practice where appropriate.

Title
Target learning objective.

Look and learn
Introduces and explains the target objective. Provides an example to illustrate it.

Practice
Provides straightforward practice activities based on the target objective.

Challenge
Provides activities to extend and challenge.

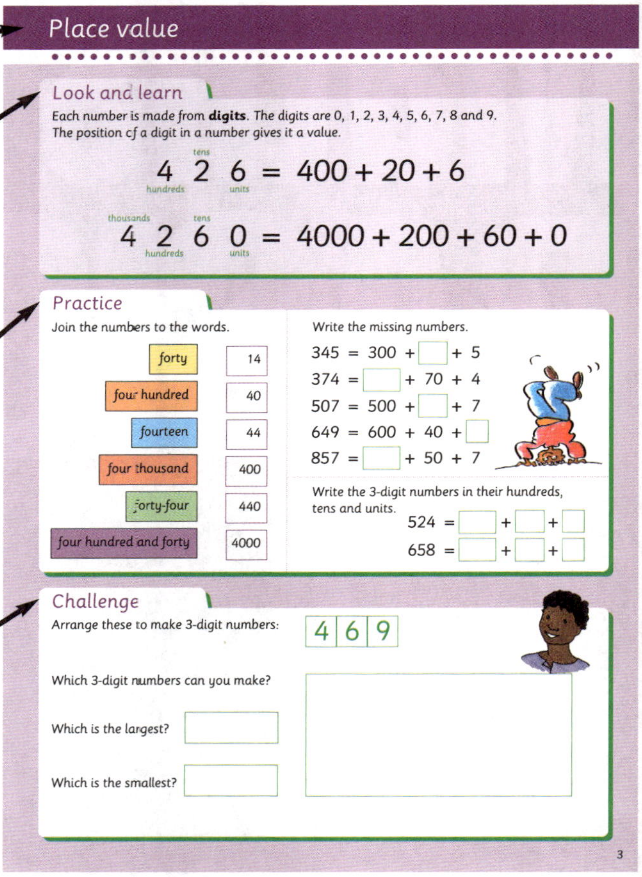
Place value

Look and learn

Each number is made from **digits**. The digits are 0, 1, 2, 3, 4, 5, 6, 7, 8 and 9.
The position of a digit in a number gives it a value.

4 2 6 = 400 + 20 + 6 (hundreds, tens, units)

4 2 6 0 = 4000 + 200 + 60 + 0 (thousands, hundreds, tens, units)

Practice

Join the numbers to the words.

forty	14
four hundred	40
fourteen	44
four thousand	400
forty-four	440
four hundred and forty	4000

Write the missing numbers.

345 = 300 + ☐ + 5
374 = ☐ + 70 + 4
507 = 500 + ☐ + 7
649 = 600 + 40 + ☐
857 = ☐ + 50 + 7

Write the 3-digit numbers in their hundreds, tens and units.

524 = ☐ + ☐ + ☐
658 = ☐ + ☐ + ☐

Challenge

Arrange these to make 3-digit numbers: 4 6 9

Which 3-digit numbers can you make?

Which is the largest?

Which is the smallest?

3

Suggested way of using the book

- It is suggested that your child works systematically through the book.
- Try tackling one unit per week.
- Read through and discuss the *Look and learn* section with your child to make sure the key objective is understood.
- Help your child get started on the Practice section.
- After this, your child can start to work fairly independently through the page, but will need further support and encouragement.
- The answers are supplied at the end of the book for checking each unit on its completion.

Enjoy the book!

Place value

Look and learn

Each number is made from **digits**. The digits are 0, 1, 2, 3, 4, 5, 6, 7, 8 and 9.
The position of a digit in a number gives it a value.

4 (hundreds) 2 (tens) 6 (units) = 400 + 20 + 6

4 (thousands) 2 (hundreds) 6 (tens) 0 (units) = 4000 + 200 + 60 + 0

Practice

Join the numbers to the words.

forty	14
four hundred	40
fourteen	44
four thousand	400
forty-four	440
four hundred and forty	4000

Write the missing numbers.

345 = 300 + ☐ + 5

374 = ☐ + 70 + 4

507 = 500 + ☐ + 7

649 = 600 + 40 + ☐

857 = ☐ + 50 + 7

Write the 3-digit numbers in their hundreds, tens and units.

524 = ☐ + ☐ + ☐

658 = ☐ + ☐ + ☐

Challenge

Arrange these to make 3-digit numbers: 4 6 9

Which 3-digit numbers can you make?

Which is the largest? ☐

Which is the smallest? ☐

Look and learn

8 + 3 **is** the same as **3 + 8**

When you add, it **does not matter** which number you start with.

8 − 3 **is not** the same as **3 − 8**

When you subtract, it **does matter** which number you start with.

Practice

Answer these.

6 + 8 = ☐	12 − 7 = ☐
7 + 7 = ☐	15 − 9 = ☐
9 + 4 = ☐	16 − 8 = ☐
12 + 6 = ☐	17 − 2 = ☐
3 + 15 = ☐	14 − 3 = ☐
4 + 13 = ☐	19 − 5 = ☐
16 + 0 = ☐	20 − 3 = ☐

Total each set of numbers.

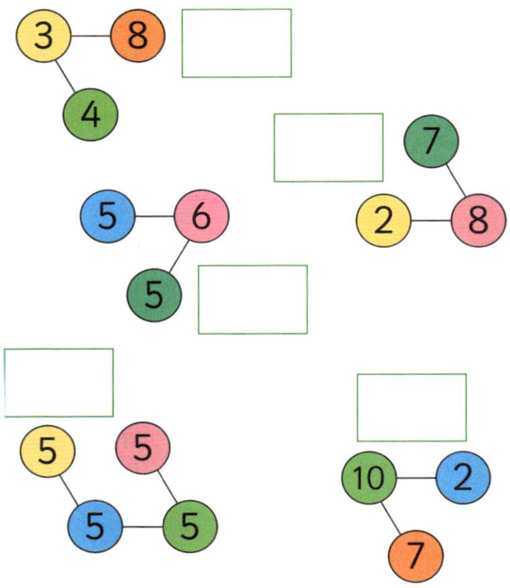

Challenge

Each triangle must total 20. Fill in the missing number.

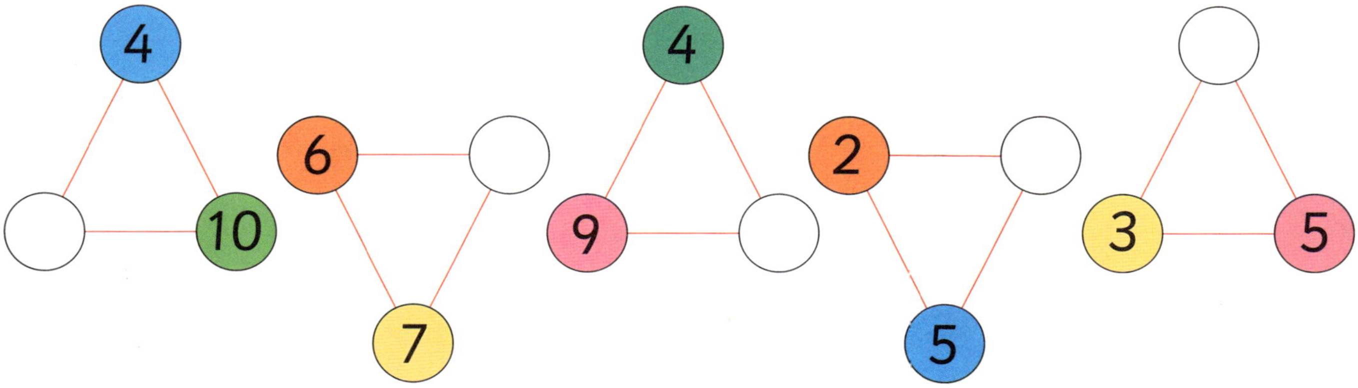

Word problems: addition and subtraction

Look and learn

Here are some **addition** words:

altogether, more, add, total, plus, sum

Here are some **subtraction** words:

subtract, leaves, take away, less, minus, difference

Practice

Answer these.

What is the sum of 4 and 8? ☐

What is the difference between 6 and 13? ☐

What is the total of 3, 5 and 7? ☐

Which number is 4 less than 17? ☐

Now answer these.

Emma has 14 stickers, Louis has 20 stickers. How many more stickers does Louis have? ☐

Julie has £1. She buys a toy for 80p. How much change should she get? ☐

Two children go swimming. It costs them 30p each. What will be the total cost? ☐

David has a 20p and a 10p coin. Hannah has a 50p and a 5p coin. How much have they altogether? ☐

Challenge

Which 3 presents can be bought for exactly £1?

Which 3 presents can be bought for exactly £1?

2D shapes

Look and learn

3-sided shapes are triangles:

4-sided shapes are quadrilaterals:

5-sided shapes are pentagons:

6-sided shapes are hexagons:

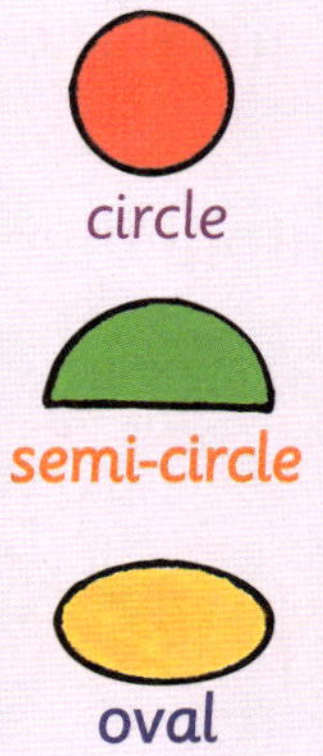

Practice

Label each shape. Draw one line of symmetry on each.

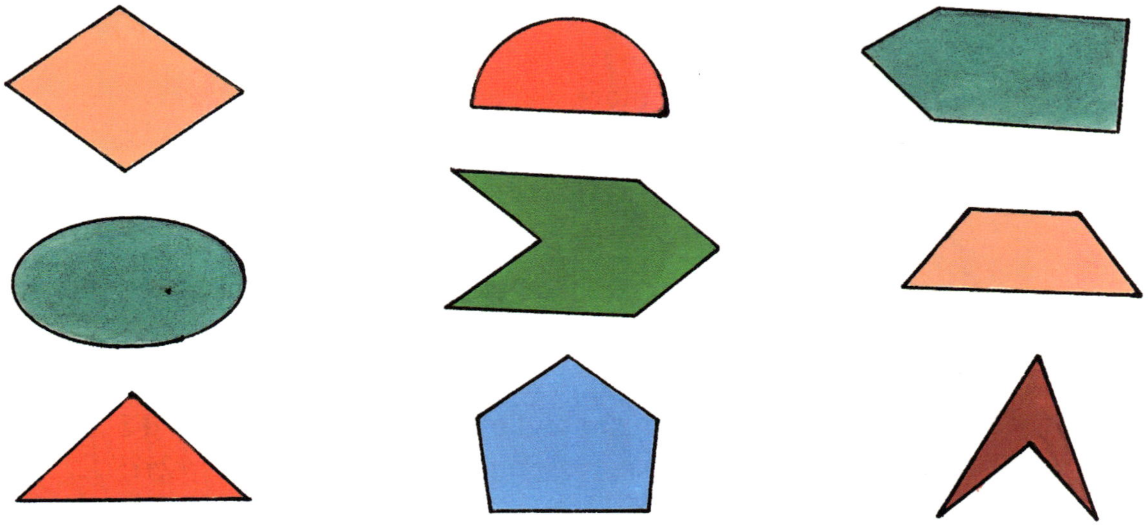

Challenge

Draw and colour the reflection of each shape.

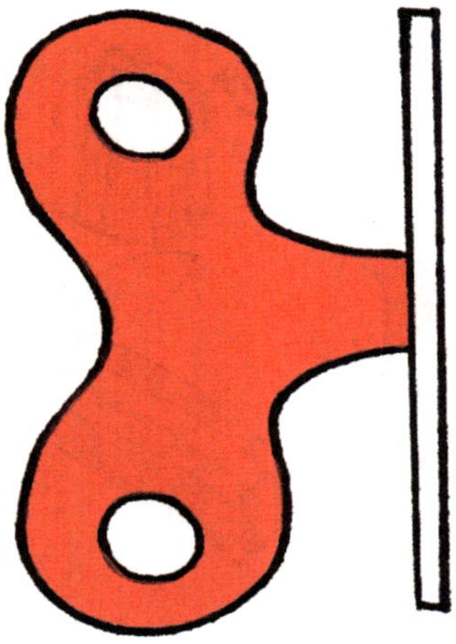

Look and learn

It is easier to **count on** *from the larger number than the smaller.*

74 + 3 is easier than 3 + 74

Practice

Add 3 to each number.

86 97 234 367

Add 1 to each number.

279 599 6099

Add 10 to each number.

279 990 6190

Write the answers.

243 + 5 =

3 + 454 =

736 + 2 =

4 + 471 =

203 + 6 =

5 + 165 =

Challenge

Look at each set of numbers and circle the odd one out. Then write why it is the odd one out.

121 56 43 97 69 145

55 95 75 15 154 135

50 75 40 450 130 260

Multiplication tables

Look and learn

Look at this multiplication table.

x	0	1	2	3	4	5	6	7	8	9	10
2	0	2	4	6	8	10	12	14	16	18	20
5	0	5	10	15	20	25	30	35	40	45	50
10	0	10	20	30	40	50	60	70	80	90	100

5 x 4 is the same as 4 x 5.
It does not matter which way you multiply them.

Practice

Answer these.

6 x 2 =
9 x 2 =
2 x 8 =
2 x 3 =
4 x 2 =
2 x 6 =
10 x 2 =

8 x 5 =
5 x 9 =
5 x 4 =
10 x 5 =
3 x 5 =
5 x 7 =
6 x 5 =

10 x 5 =
10 x 9 =
7 x 10 =
8 x 10 =
5 x 10 =
10 x 9 =
10 x 10 =

Challenge

Fill in the missing numbers.

 x 2 = 18

 x 4 = 8

 x 10 = 90

7 x  = 35

9 x  = 45

10 x  = 70

 x 10 = 50

6 x  = 12

8 x  = 40

Look and learn

Look at these different sorts of money.

coins

notes

Practice

Work out the change in each case.

price	money given	change
65p		
75p		
£1.50		
£2.50		
£5.50		

Add these prices.

prices		total
60p	35p	
75p	25p	
£1.50	£2	
£4	£3.50	
80p	80p	

Challenge

Which 3 coins will total 27p?

Which 3 coins will total 72p?

Which 3 coins will total 90p?

Look and learn

Look at these fractions.

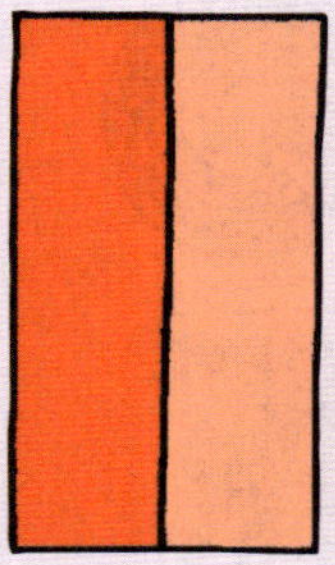

half

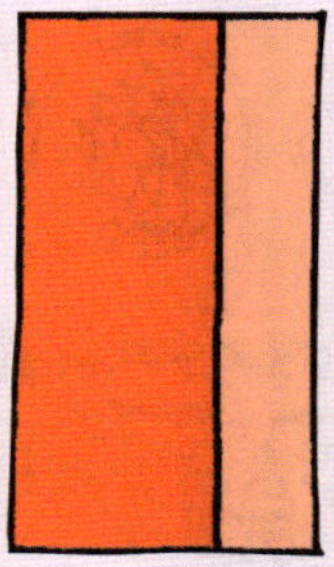

not a half

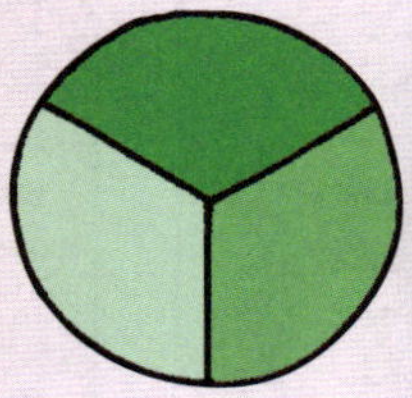

thirds

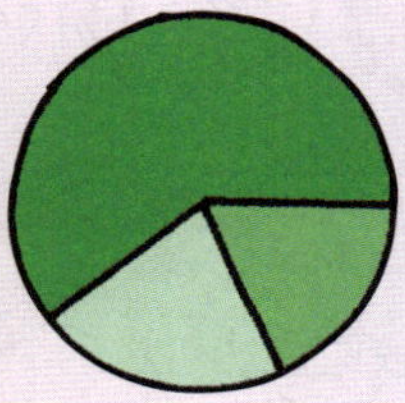

not thirds

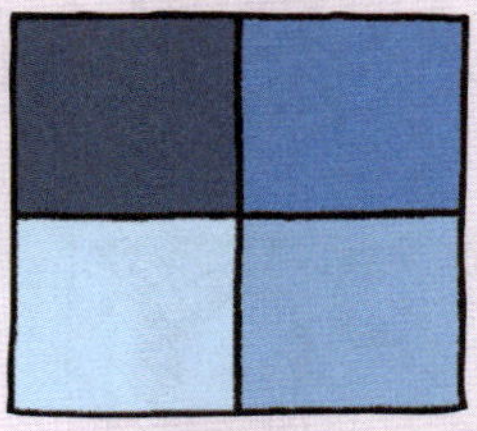

quarters

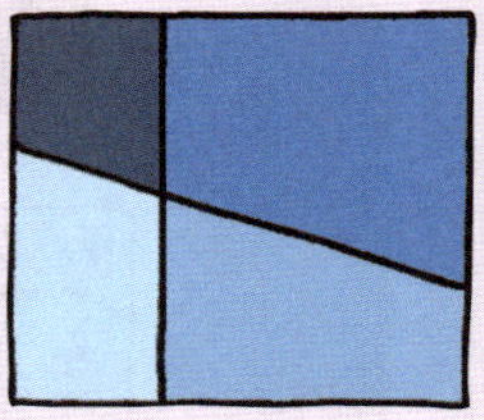

not quarters

Practice

Name the fractions coloured red.

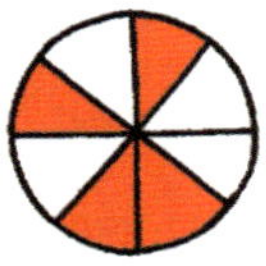

....

....

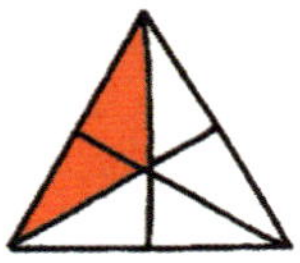

....

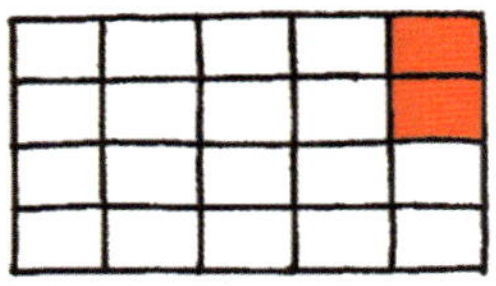

....

What is $\frac{1}{2}$ of 12? ....

What is $\frac{1}{3}$ of 12? ....

What is $\frac{1}{4}$ of 12? ....

What is $\frac{1}{2}$ of 20? ....

What is $\frac{1}{4}$ of 20? ....

What is $\frac{1}{10}$ of 20? ....

Challenge

Colour in the fractions of these wholes.

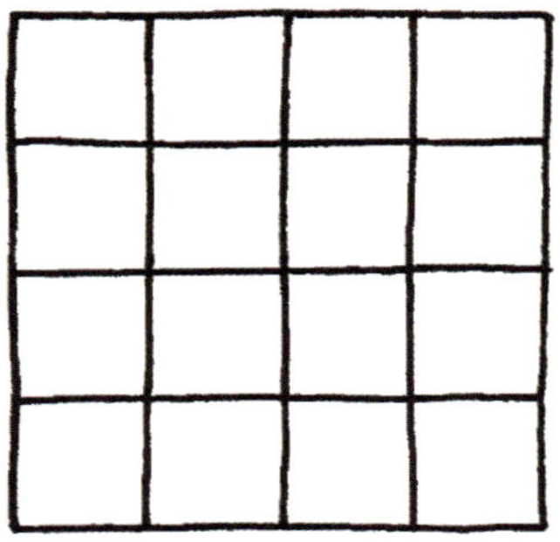

colour $\frac{1}{4}$

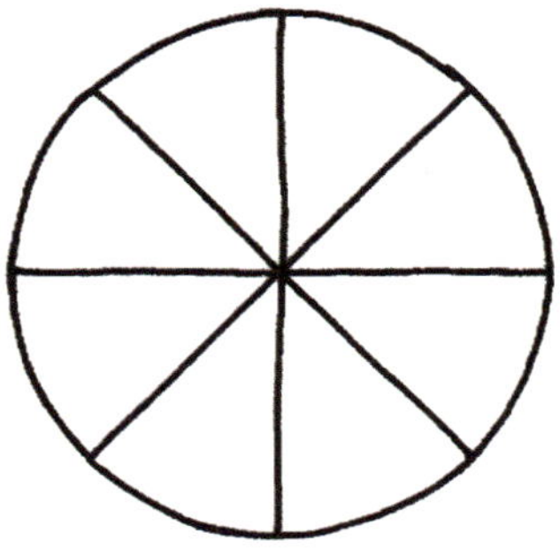

colour $\frac{3}{4}$

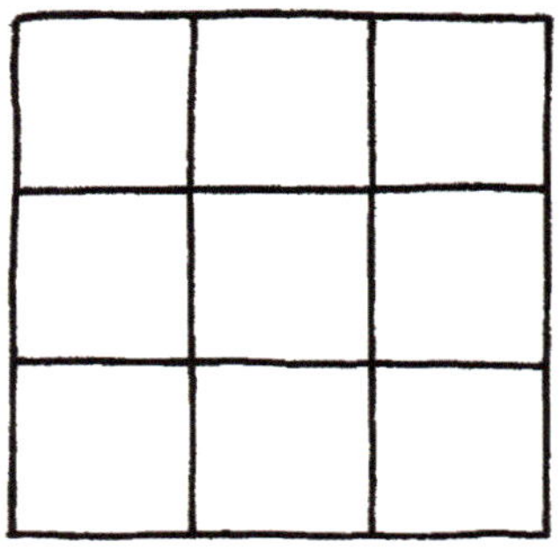

colour $\frac{1}{3}$

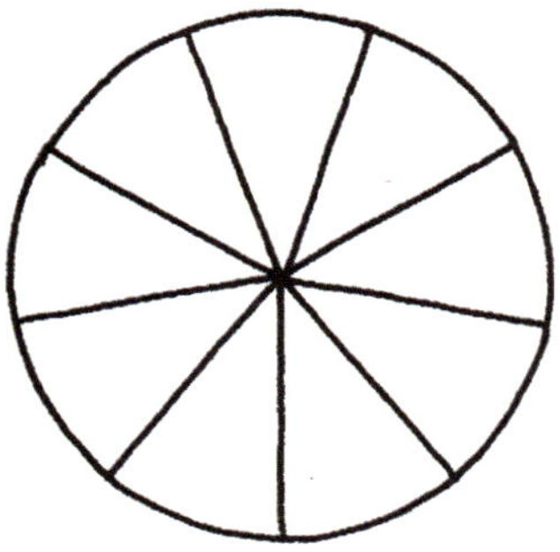

colour $\frac{2}{3}$

Look and learn

Look at these minutes past the hour.

Practice

Fill in the times.

Challenge

How many minutes are in 1 hour? ....

Which month follows August? ....

How many days are there in March? ....

What time is half an hour after 3.15? ....

If it is 2.35, how long is it until 3.00? ....

Data handling

Look and learn

Properties of shapes are things such as:

right angles
number of sides
curves
colour

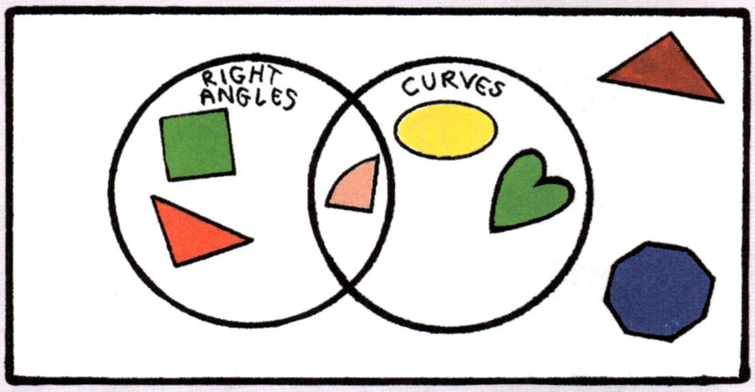

The crossover part must match both properties.

Practice

Draw arrows to show where each shape goes.

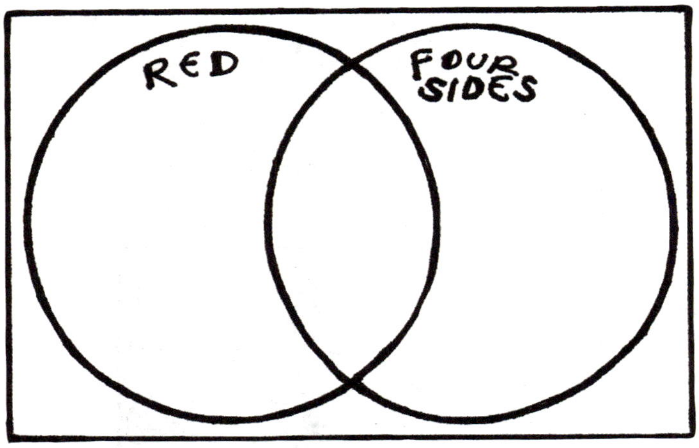

Challenge

Draw arrows to show where each shape goes.

	green	not green
right angles		
not right angles		

Rounding and scales

Look and learn

Learn rounding to the nearest hundred.

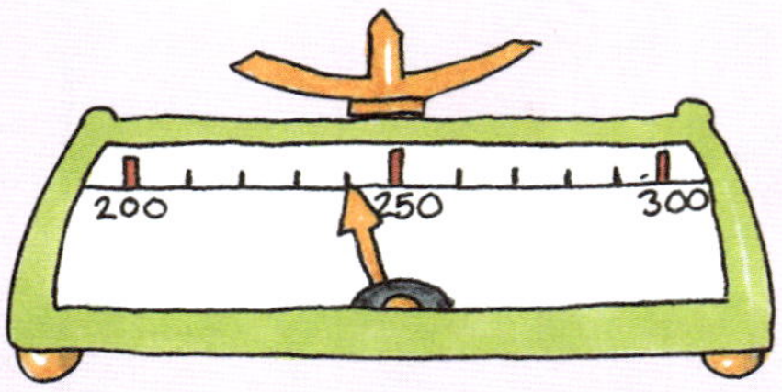

240 is nearer to 200 than 300.
It is **rounded down** to 200.

560 is nearer to 600 than 500.
It is **rounded up** to 600.

850 is half-way between 800 and 900.
It is **rounded up** to 900.

Practice

Round each number to the nearest 10.

54 ≈ ___ 75 ≈ ___

68 ≈ ___ 99 ≈ ___

33 ≈ ___ 57 ≈ ___

Round each number to the nearest 100.

140 ≈ ___ 380 ≈ ___

850 ≈ ___ 420 ≈ ___

Read each of these scales.

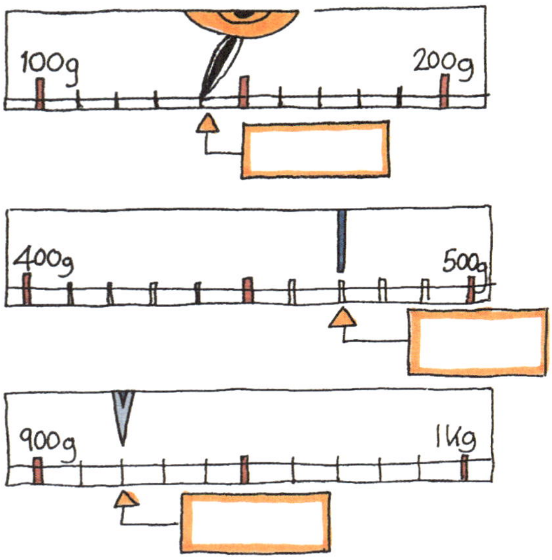

Challenge

Write each set of measures in order of size.
Start with the smallest.

760g 670g 730g

....

690g 609g 906g

....

Read each of these scales.

Look and learn

Here is a useful addition trick.

36 + 29 — this is 30 − 1

So a quick way to work it out is:

36 + 30 → then −1 = 65

And:

46 + 28

= ↓ ↓ =

40 + 6 + 20 + 8 = 74

There are lots of ways to add up numbers. This is just one way.

Practice

Do these quickly in your head.

60 + 40 = ☐

30 + 50 = ☐

80 + 80 = ☐

60 + 70 = ☐

60 + 39 = ☐

30 + 49 = ☐

80 + 79 = ☐

60 + 69 = ☐

8 + 7 + 9 = ☐

20 + 30 + 50 = ☐

42 + 58 = ☐

37 + 48 = ☐

65 + 86 = ☐

77 + 77 = ☐

Challenge

Write the numbers that go into and come out of the number machines.

in	56			99
out		97	84	

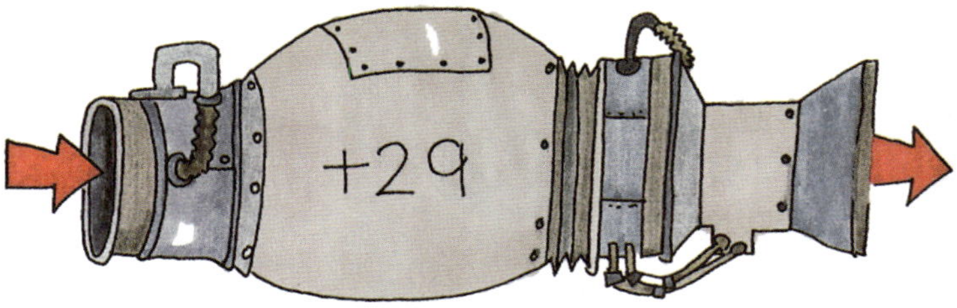

in	65		95	
out		55		40

Word problems: multiplication and division

Look and learn

Here are some **multiplication** words:

multiply, lots of, product, times, multiple

Here are some **division** words:

divide, share, remainder, factor, quotient

Practice

Answer these.

What is the product of 5 and 10?

What is 30 divided by 5?

What is 2 multiplied by 9?

What is the quotient of 12 and 2?

Now try these.

Gita has 9 stamps. Paul has twice as many. How many stamps has Paul?

Each eggbox holds 10 eggs. There are 80 eggs. How many boxes are needed?

A book costs £5. How much will 7 books cost?

Pencils cost 5p each. How many can Leroy buy with 40p?

Challenge

A car holds 5 people. How many cars will be needed for 22 people?

If 17p is shared equally between 2 people, how much will each receive and how much will be left over?

Three people have 5p each. Four people have 10p each. How much is that altogether?

Look and learn

Look at these shapes. Do you recognise any of them?

This is a sphere.

← These are all prisms. →

This is a hemisphere.

Practice

Join the shapes up to the words that describe them.

prism

not a prism

curved face

not curved face

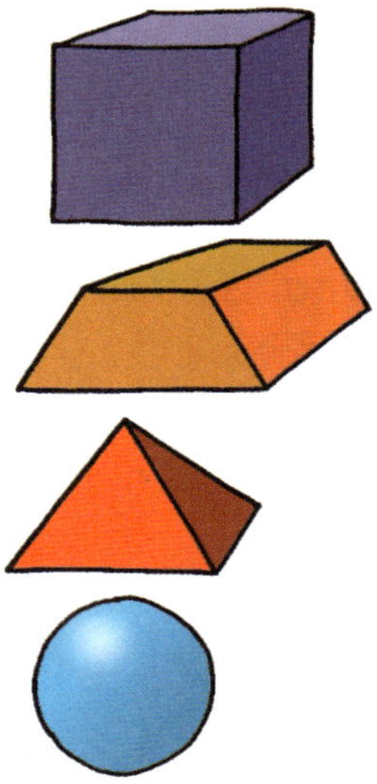

Challenge

Which of these statements are true and which are false?

1. A hemisphere has a flat face.

____

2. A cube's faces are all square.

____

3. A prism has a rectangular face.

____

4. A cuboid has a triangular face.

____

5. A sphere has a flat face.

____

6. A cone has a circular face.

____

Look and learn

It is useful to know measurements that are the same.

1 metre = 100 centimetres 1m = 100cm	1 litre = 1000 millilitres 1l = 1000ml	1 kilogram = 1000 grammes 1 kg = 1000g
1 kilometre = 1000 metres 1km = 1000m		

Practice

Answer these.

$\frac{1}{2}$ metre = ☐ cm

$\frac{1}{2}$ kilogram = ☐ g

$\frac{1}{2}$ litre = ☐ ml

$\frac{1}{2}$ kilometre = ☐ m

$\frac{1}{2}$ hour = ☐ minutes

$\frac{1}{2}$ minute = ☐ seconds

Write these times.

Challenge

Use a ruler to measure each line to the nearest $\frac{1}{2}$ cm.

1. ______________ ☐

2. ______________ ☐

3. ______________ ☐

4. ______________ ☐

5. ______________ ☐

6. ______________ ☐

7. ______________ ☐

Numbers: odd and even

Look and learn

Odd numbers end in 1, 3, 5, 7 or 9.

Even numbers end in 0, 2, 4, 6 or 8.

'0' on its own stands for **nothing**. It is neither odd nor even.

Practice

Fill in the missing numbers to continue the patterns.

33	43	53				
245	255	265				
96	86	76				
542	532	522				
125	225	325				
904	804	704				

Circle the odd numbers in these patterns.

Challenge

Which is the next odd number after 45?

Which is the next even number after 68?

Which even numbers are between 31 and 35?

Which odd numbers are between 52 and 56?

Multiplication and division

Look and learn

Doubling is the same as **multiplying by 2**.

double 12 =

12 + 12 or

2 x 12

Halving is the same as **dividing by 2**.

halve 20 =

$20 \div 2$

Practice

I double each number I visit. Fill in the answers.

16 →

35 →

60 →

250 →

I halve each number I visit. Fill in the answers.

£8 →

20kg →

12km →

16cm →

Challenge

Write the numbers that go into and come out of these number machines.

in	12			20
out		20	30	

in	20			40
out		15	25	

Money

Look and learn

There are 100 pence in a pound, so:

£3·25 = 325 pence

450 pence = £4·50

£5 = £5·00 (decimal point)

When describing money with numbers, there are **always** 2 digits after the **decimal point**.

Practice

Total each amount.

= £

= £

= £

= £

= £

Write how many pennies.

Challenge

Leon buys 2 books. They cost £2 and £2.20. How much change will he receive from £5?

Alexis bought a CD. She had 20p change from a £10 note. How much was her CD?

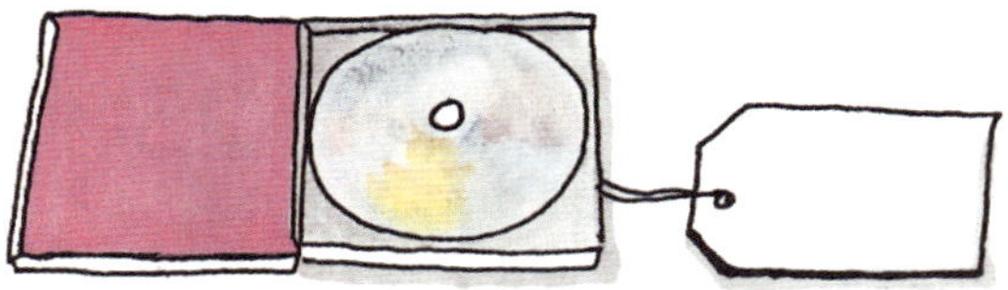

Which 2 items when bought together will cost £5?

What will be the total cost of all 3 items?

Fractions

Look and learn

Look at these fractions.

wholes

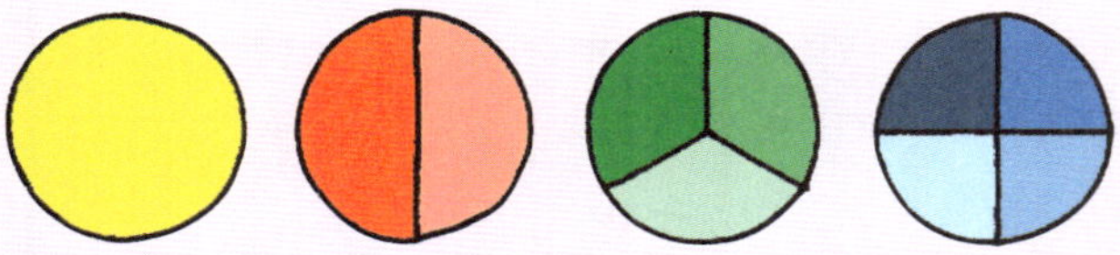

$1 \quad \frac{2}{2} \quad \frac{3}{3} \quad \frac{4}{4}$

halves

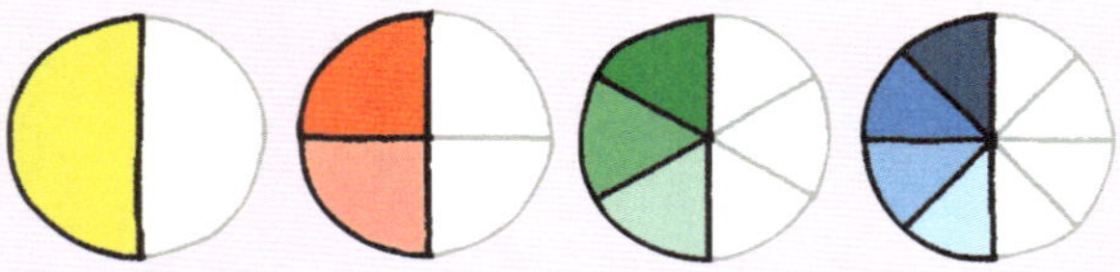

$\frac{1}{2} \quad \frac{2}{4} \quad \frac{3}{6} \quad \frac{4}{8}$

Practice

Which fraction of each flag is coloured red?

Which fraction of each item is coloured green? Put a cross next to the odd one out.

Challenge

Colour half the number of circles on each shield.
Make each half look different.

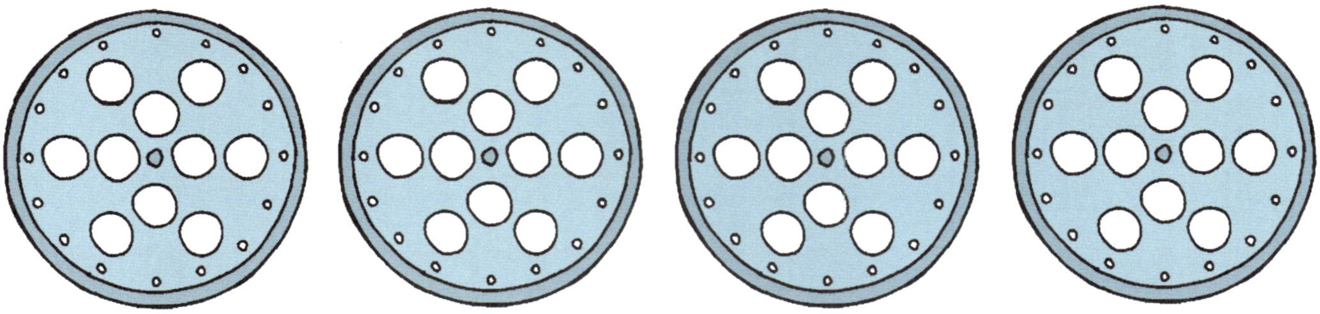

How many tenths are there in a half? ☐

Look and learn

Some information is put in **tables**.

The **rows** give us some information.

The **columns** give us other information.

Practice

Here are 4 shopping baskets.

Study the baskets. Fill in the information in the table below.

	boxes	bags	tins	bottles/jars	total items
Ali family	1				
Sudbury family					
Williams family			2		
Poggio family					
Total					

Place value and rounding

Look and learn

Rounding to tens and hundreds.

Round **up** if the number is half-way or after.
Round **down** if it is not half-way.

Round **up** if the number is half-way or after.
Round **down** if it is not half-way.

Practice

In the first box, write the number indicated by the arrow. In the second, write its **rounded** number. The symbol ≈ means **approximately**.

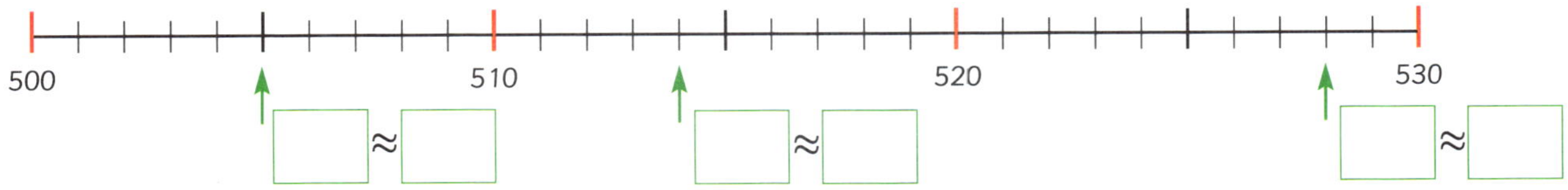

Round numbers to the nearest 10.

Round numbers to the nearest 100.

Challenge

Join each number to its nearest 100.

250 194 574 650 912

100 — 200 — 300 — 400 — 500 — 600 — 700 — 800 — 900 — 1000

149 218 375 625 985

Look and learn

Here is a useful subtraction trick.

46 – 29 (this is 30 – 1)

So a quick way to work it out is:

46 – 30 → then +1 = 17

Or count up: 54 – 26

answer = 28

There are lots of ways to subtract numbers.

Practice

Do these quickly in your head

90 – 40 =

80 – 60 =

140 – 50 =

120 – 80 =

70 – 29 =

50 – 19 =

80 – 49 =

90 – 69 =

Subtract the second number from the first.

34 16 =

42 17 =

55 28 =

64 36 =

87 58 =

74 36 =

Challenge

Make each scale total 100.

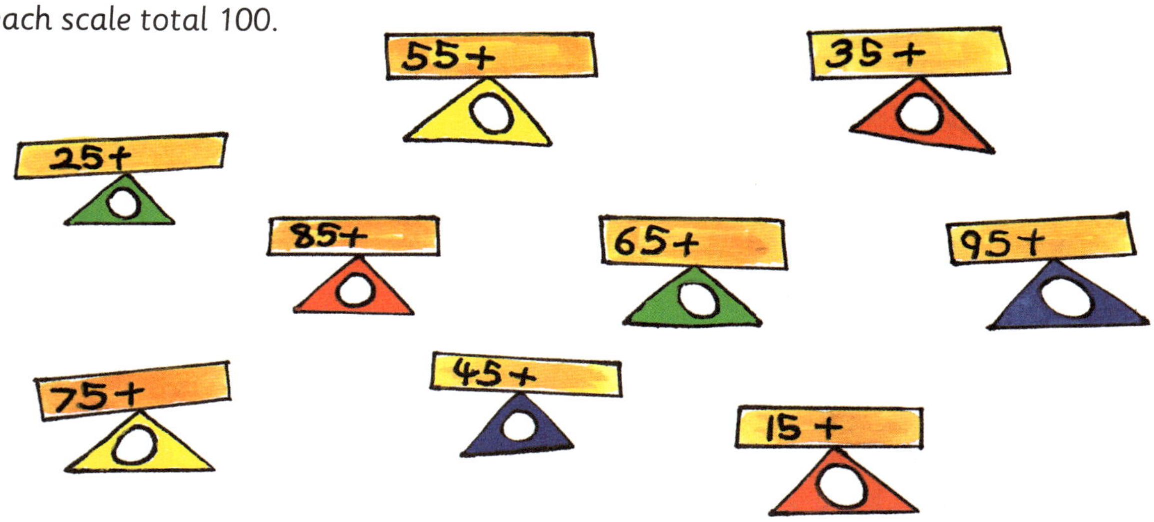

Money problems

Practice

6 eggs cost 36p.
What is the cost of 12 eggs?

Apples cost 70p for a kilogram.
What is the cost of half a kilogram?

Milk costs 25p for a carton.
How many cartons can be bought for £2?

Practice

a 

b 

c 

d 

What is the total cost of b, c and d?

What would 2 each of c and a cost?

How much change would you get from 50p if b and d are bought?

Challenge

Which **two** coins would you offer to pay for these?

80p + 50p

£1·50 + £1·30

£1·75 + 40p

Shape: right angles

Look and learn

It is useful to recognise right angles.

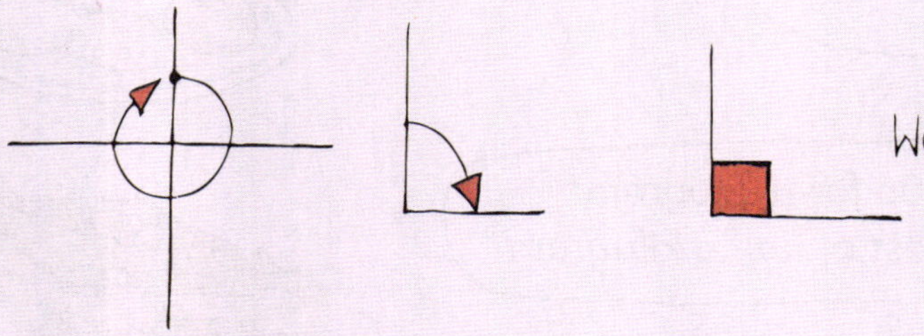

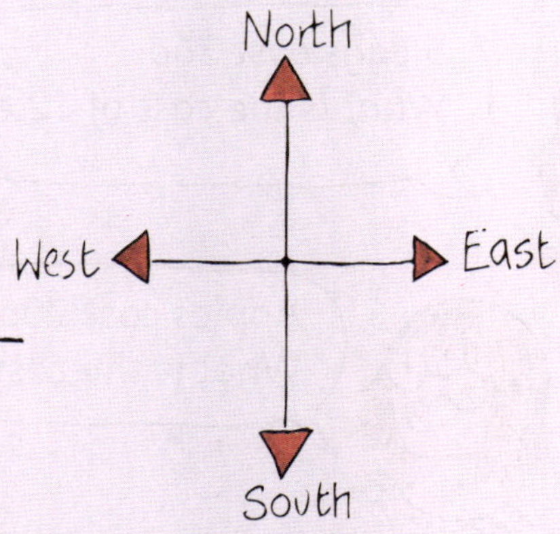

Practice

Tick each right angle.

Look at the angles on each shape.
Tick the right angles.

Challenge

Follow the compass instructions.

Face N

Make $\frac{1}{4}$ turn clockwise.
Where do you face?

....

Face E

Make $\frac{1}{2}$ turn clockwise.
Where do you face?

....

Face W

Make $\frac{1}{4}$ turn anticlockwise.
Where do you face?

....

Face S

Make $\frac{3}{4}$ turn anticlockwise.
Where do you face?

....

Counting and estimating

Look and learn

This symbol ≈ means **approximately**.

So, $129 \approx 130$

An **estimate** is a **sensible guess**.

There are either 4, 40, or 400 bees in the hive. Which is the best estimate?

Practice

Tick the best estimate of bees in each hive.

20

80

100

10

50

500

14

140

1400

Fill in the missing numbers.

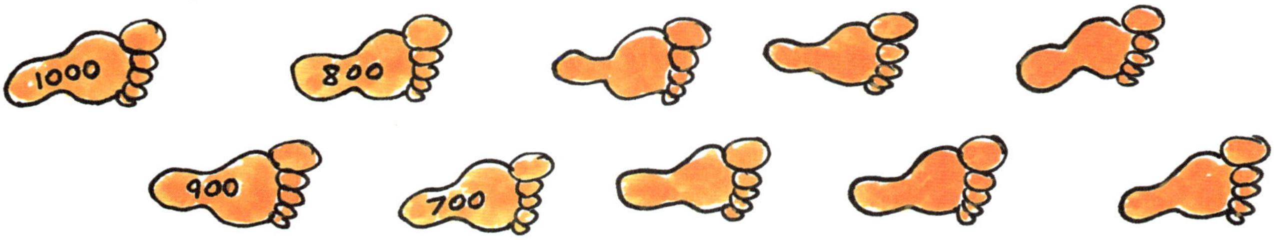

Challenge

Draw more hops to continue the sequence. Fill in the numbers where the bee lands.

Look and learn

This is the division sign

÷

4 twos

8 ÷ 2

How many twos in 8?

Practice

How many twos in 10?

10 ÷ 2 =

How many twos in 14?

14 ÷ 2 =

How many fives in 15?

15 ÷ 5 =

How many threes in 9?

9 ÷ 3 =

Challenge

How many twos in 11?

11 ÷ 2 = remainder?

How many fives in 12?

12 ÷ 5 = remainder?

How many threes in 11?

11 ÷ 3 = remainder?

Practice

5 stickers costs 30p
What would 1 sticker cost?

Stamps cost 10p each.
What would 8 stamps cost?

Pencils cost 19p each.
What would 3 pencils cost?

Crayons cost 36p a packet.
How much change would you have from 50p?

The time is 3:15.
What time will it be in half an hour?

What is the time an hour before 3:50?

The time is 2:40.
How many minutes will pass before it is 4:00?

Challenge

Ian baked 18 strawberry tarts and 16 lemon tarts.

How many tarts were baked altogether?

How many strawberry tarts would be left if half of them were eaten?

How many lemon tarts would be left if half of them were eaten?

How many tarts have been eaten if only 8 tarts are left altogther?

Look and learn

Look at these *fractions* of things.

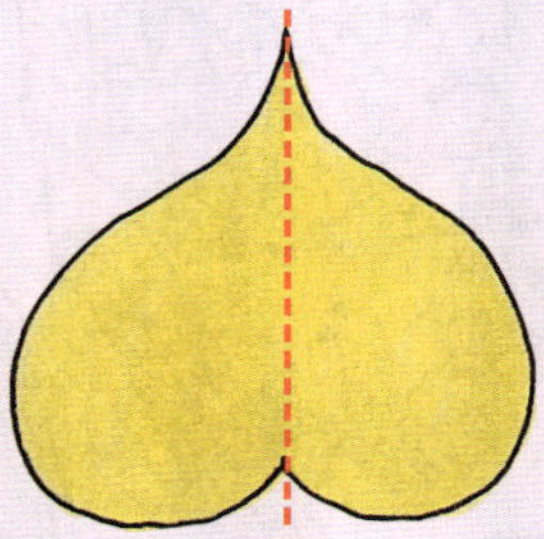

$\frac{1}{2}$ a shape

$\frac{1}{2}$ a quantity

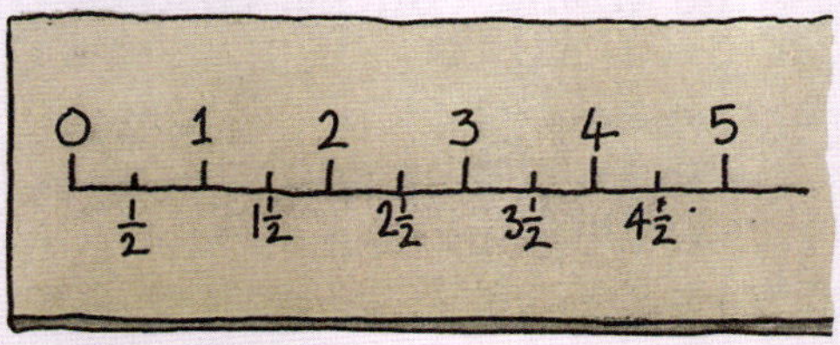

$\frac{1}{2}$ a number on the line

Practice

Draw a line to show $\frac{1}{2}$ *of* each shape.

Draw lines to show $\frac{1}{4}$ *of* each shape.

Circle $\frac{1}{2}$ *of* each set.

Challenge

Write the *fraction* to which each arrow points.

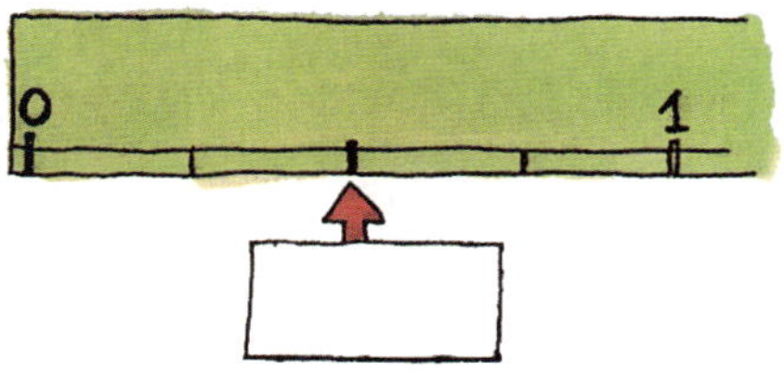

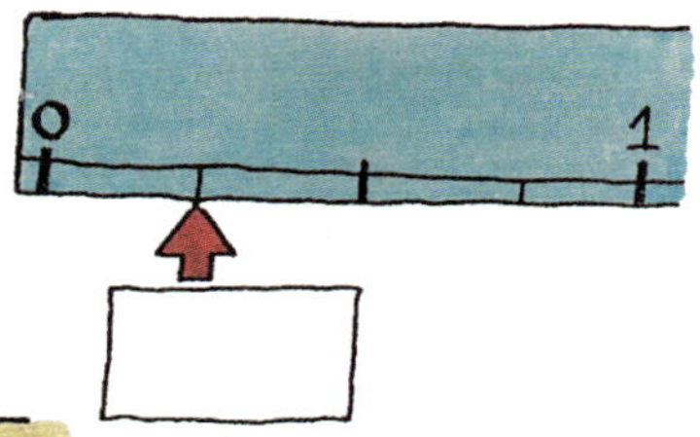

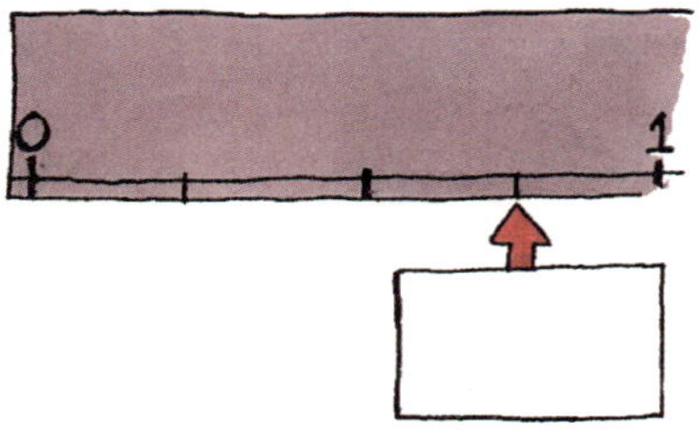

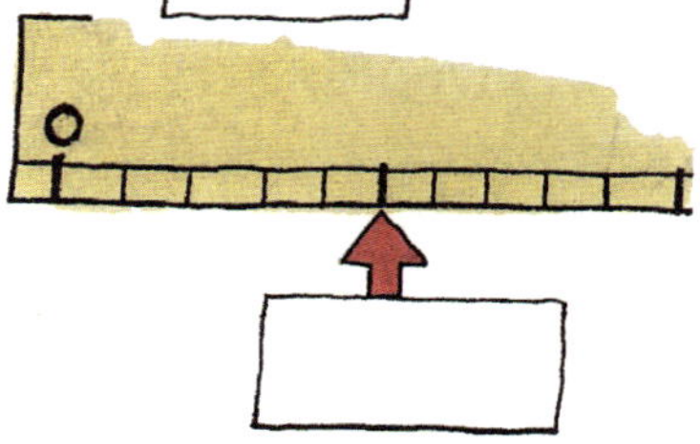

Look and learn

A calendar shows **12 months**. It also shows **dates**.

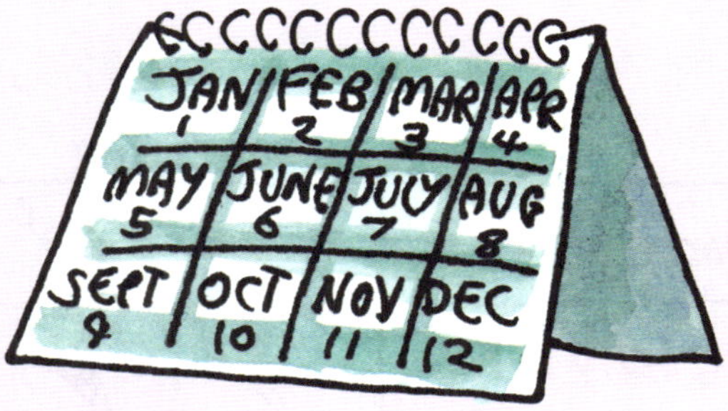

A date consists of:

Practice

On which day is May 3rd?

Which date is the 3rd Saturday in May?

Which date is 1 week later than May 22nd?

On which day is June 2nd?

Challenge

Look at the children's badges.

Who is the oldest?

Who is the youngest?

Who was born on the 7th month?

Who was born after August?

Practice

Here is a graph about favourite ice creams.

How many children liked banana best?

How many children liked raspberry ripple best?

Which flavour was most popular?

Which flavour was least popular?

How many children were asked about ice cream altogether?

Challenge

Children's pastimes

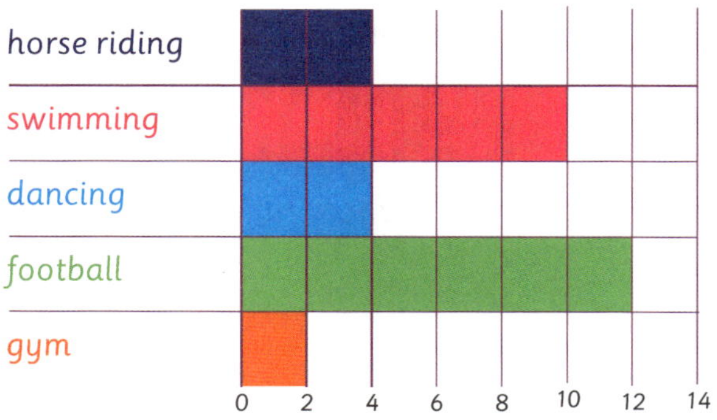

How many went dancing?

Which was the most popular activity?

Which two activities were enjoyed by the same number of children?

Which activity was enjoyed by the fewest children?

How many children were asked altogether?